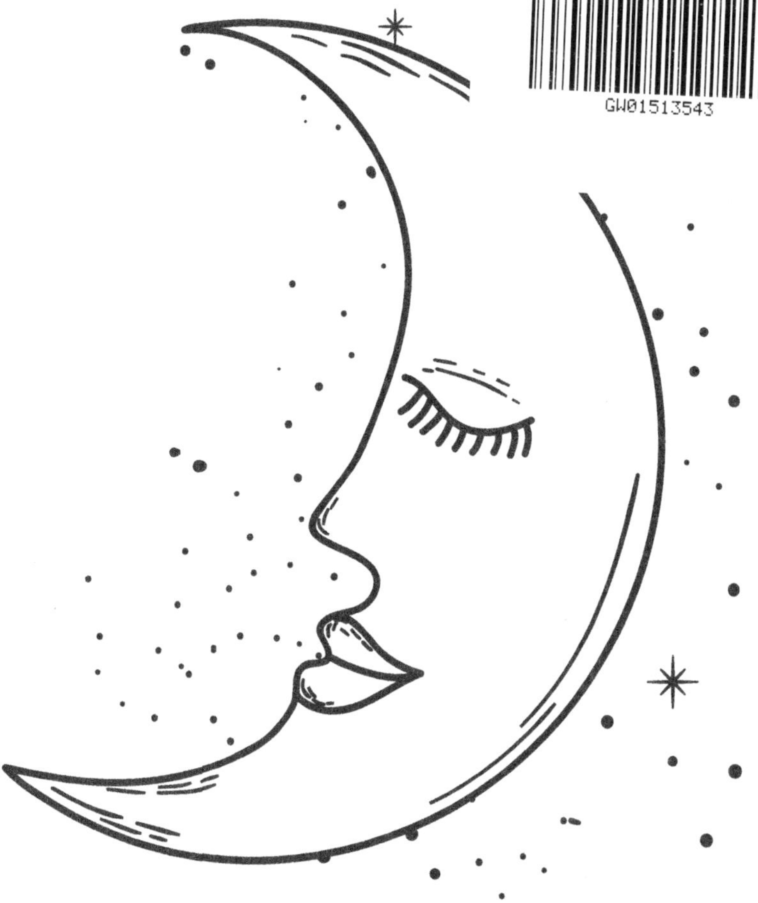

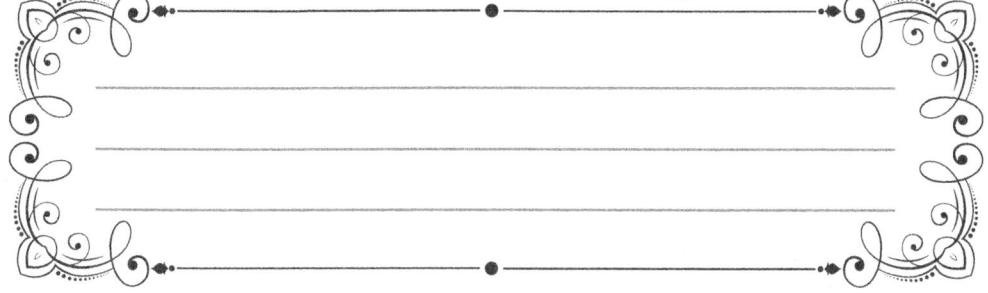

This Journal belongs to:

Copyright © 2021 Maniclout Press

All Rights Reserved, no part of this book may be used or reproduced by any means, graphic, electronic, or mechanical, including photocopying, recording, taping, or by any information storage retrieval system without the written permission of the publisher

MOOD TRACKER

A daily diary to help you track your mood, make goals to acheive, practice gratitude and promote positive thinking everyday. Each journal has two entries for each day - The first for the morning and the second for the evening.

The Morning entry page contains the following:

- Section to note hours slept the previous night.
- Section to rank energy levels from 1-5.
- Section to track your mood.
- Space to write three things you're grateful for today.
- Space to write three goals to achieve today.

The Evening entry page contains the following:

- Section to note how many goals were achieved.
- 2nd Section to rank your energy levels in the evening.
- 2nd Section to to track your mood once again.
- Section to note three positive things about your day
- Space for a journal entry - to go into a little more detail about your day, if you wish!

If you find this Journal helpful, let others know by leaving a review on Amazon!

Today's date is ___/___/___

MORNING ENTRY

Hours Slept

Energy Level
1 - 5

Today I Feel...?

Three things im grateful for :

1. _____
2. _____
3. _____

Three goals for today :

1. _____
2. _____
3. _____

EVENING ENTRY

Goals Met
1 - 3

Energy Level
1 - 5

This Evening I Feel...?

Today I was anxious about...

_____
_____
_____
_____

Three positive things about my day were...

1 _____
2 _____
3 _____

Journal Entry/Free Space...

_____
_____
_____
_____
_____

Today's date is ___/___/___

MORNING ENTRY

Hours Slept

Energy Level
1 - 5

Today I Feel...?

Three things im grateful for :

1. _____
2. _____
3. _____

Three goals for today :

1. _____
2. _____
3. _____

EVENING ENTRY

Goals Met
1 - 3

Energy Level
1 - 5

This Evening I Feel...?

Today I was anxious about...

_____
_____
_____
_____

Three positive things about my day were...

1 _____
2 _____
3 _____

Journal Entry/Free Space...

_____
_____
_____
_____
_____

Today's date is ___/___/___

MORNING ENTRY

Hours Slept

Energy Level
1 - 5

Today I Feel...?

Three things i'm grateful for :

1. _____
2. _____
3. _____

Three goals for today :

1. _____
2. _____
3. _____

EVENING ENTRY

Goals Met
1 - 3

Energy Level
1 - 5

This Evening I Feel...?

Today I was anxious about...

Three positive things about my day were...
1
2
3

Journal Entry/Free Space...

Today's date is ___/___/___

MORNING ENTRY

Hours Slept

Energy Level
1 - 5

Today I Feel...?

Three things im grateful for :

1. _____
2. _____
3. _____

Three goals for today :

1. _____
2. _____
3. _____

EVENING ENTRY

Goals Met
1 - 3

Energy Level
1 - 5

This Evening I Feel...?

Today I was anxious about...

_____
_____
_____
_____

Three positive things about my day were...

1. _____
2. _____
3. _____

Journal Entry/Free Space...

_____
_____
_____
_____
_____

Today's date is ___/___/___

MORNING ENTRY

Hours Slept

Energy Level
1 - 5

Today I Feel...?

Three things im grateful for :

1. _____
2. _____
3. _____

Three goals for today :

1. _____
2. _____
3. _____

EVENING ENTRY

Goals Met
1 - 3

Energy Level
1 - 5

This Evening I Feel...?

Today I was anxious about...

_____
_____
_____
_____

Three positive things about my day were...

1 _____
2 _____
3 _____

Journal Entry/Free Space...

_____
_____
_____
_____

Today's date is ___/___/___

MORNING ENTRY

Hours Slept

Energy Level
1 - 5

Today I Feel...?

Three things im grateful for :

1 _____
2 _____
3 _____

Three goals for today :

1 _____
2 _____
3 _____

EVENING ENTRY

Goals Met
1 - 3

Energy Level
1 - 5

This Evening I Feel...?

Today I was anxious about...

_____
_____
_____
_____

Three positive things about my day were...

1 _____
2 _____
3 _____

Journal Entry/Free Space...

_____
_____
_____
_____
_____

Today's date is ___/___/___

MORNING ENTRY

Hours Slept

Energy Level
1 - 5

Today I Feel...?

Three things im grateful for :

1. _____
2. _____
3. _____

Three goals for today :

1. _____
2. _____
3. _____

EVENING ENTRY

Goals Met
1 - 3

Energy Level
1 - 5

This Evening I Feel...?

Today I was anxious about...

_____
_____
_____
_____

Three positive things about my day were...

1 _____
2 _____
3 _____

Journal Entry/Free Space...

_____
_____
_____
_____
_____

Today's date is ___/___/___

MORNING ENTRY

Hours Slept

Energy Level
1 - 5

Today I Feel...?

Three things im grateful for :

1. _____
2. _____
3. _____

Three goals for today :

1. _____
2. _____
3. _____

EVENING ENTRY

Goals Met
1 - 3

Energy Level
1 - 5

This Evening I Feel...?

Today I was anxious about...

___

___

___

Three positive things about my day were...

1 ___
2 ___
3 ___

Journal Entry/Free Space...

___

___

___

___

___

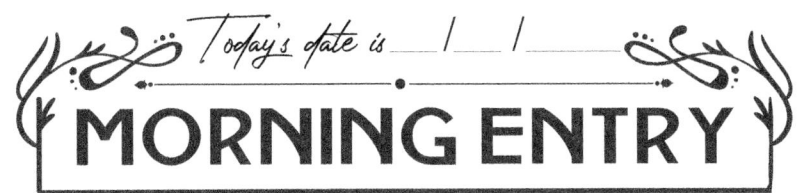

Today's date is ___/___/___

MORNING ENTRY

Hours Slept

Energy Level 1 - 5

Today I Feel...?

Three things im grateful for :

1. _____
2. _____
3. _____

Three goals for today :

1. _____
2. _____
3. _____

EVENING ENTRY

Goals Met
1 - 3

Energy Level
1 - 5

This Evening I Feel...?

Today I was anxious about...
_____
_____
_____

Three positive things about my day were...
1 _____
2 _____
3 _____

Journal Entry/Free Space...
_____
_____
_____
_____

Today's date is ___/___/___

MORNING ENTRY

Hours Slept | **Energy Level** 1 - 5 | **Today I Feel...?**

Three things im grateful for :

1. _____
2. _____
3. _____

Three goals for today :

1. _____
2. _____
3. _____

EVENING ENTRY

Goals Met
1 - 3

Energy Level
1 - 5

This Evening I Feel...?

Today I was anxious about...

_____
_____
_____

Three positive things about my day were...

1 _____
2 _____
3 _____

Journal Entry/Free Space...

_____
_____
_____
_____
_____

Today's date is ___/___/___

MORNING ENTRY

Hours Slept

Energy Level
1 - 5

Today I Feel...?

Three things im grateful for :

1. _____
2. _____
3. _____

Three goals for today :

1. _____
2. _____
3. _____

EVENING ENTRY

Goals Met
1 - 3

Energy Level
1 - 5

This Evening I Feel...?

Today I was anxious about...

Three positive things about my day were...

1
2
3

Journal Entry/Free Space...

Today's date is ___/___/___

MORNING ENTRY

Hours Slept

Energy Level
1 - 5

Today I Feel...?

Three things im grateful for :

1. _____
2. _____
3. _____

Three goals for today :

1. _____
2. _____
3. _____

EVENING ENTRY

Goals Met
1 - 3

Energy Level
1 - 5

This Evening I Feel...?

Today I was anxious about...

_____
_____
_____
_____

Three positive things about my day were...

1. _____
2. _____
3. _____

Journal Entry/Free Space...

_____
_____
_____
_____
_____

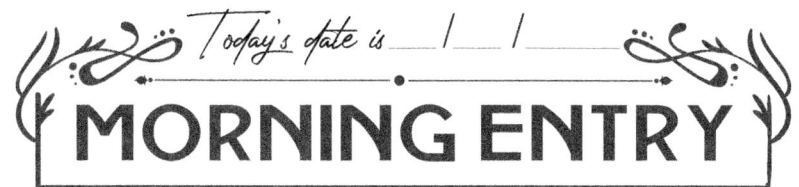

Today's date is ___/___/___

MORNING ENTRY

Hours Slept

Energy Level
1 - 5

Today I Feel...?

Three things im grateful for:

1. _____
_____
2. _____
_____
3. _____
_____

Three goals for today:

1. _____
_____
2. _____
_____
3. _____
_____

EVENING ENTRY

Goals Met
1 - 3

Energy Level
1 - 5

This Evening I Feel...?

Today I was anxious about...

_____
_____
_____
_____

Three positive things about my day were...

1 _____
2 _____
3 _____

Journal Entry/Free Space...

_____
_____
_____
_____
_____

Today's date is ___/___/___

MORNING ENTRY

| Hours Slept | Energy Level 1-5 | Today I Feel...? |

Three things I'm grateful for :

1. _____
2. _____
3. _____

Three goals for today :

1. _____
2. _____
3. _____

EVENING ENTRY

Goals Met
1 - 3

Energy Level
1 - 5

This Evening I Feel...?

Today I was anxious about...

___

Three positive things about my day were...

1.
2.
3.

Journal Entry/Free Space...

Today's date is ___/___/___

MORNING ENTRY

Hours Slept

Energy Level
1 - 5

Today I Feel...?

Three things im grateful for:

1. _____
2. _____
3. _____

Three goals for today:

1. _____
2. _____
3. _____

EVENING ENTRY

Goals Met
1 - 3

Energy Level
1 - 5

This Evening I Feel...?

Today I was anxious about...

___

Three positive things about my day were...
1
2
3

Journal Entry/Free Space...

Today's date is ___/___/___

MORNING ENTRY

Hours Slept

Energy Level
1 - 5

Today I Feel...?

Three things im grateful for :

1. _____
2. _____
3. _____

Three goals for today :

1. _____
2. _____
3. _____

EVENING ENTRY

Goals Met	Energy Level	This Evening I Feel...?
1 - 3	1 - 5	

Today I was anxious about...

_____
_____
_____
_____

Three positive things about my day were...

1. _____
2. _____
3. _____

Journal Entry/Free Space...

_____
_____
_____
_____
_____

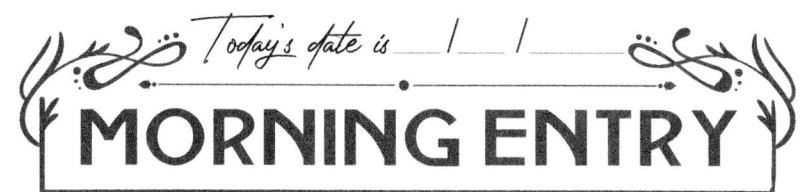

Today's date is ___/___/___

MORNING ENTRY

Hours Slept

Energy Level
1 - 5

Today I Feel...?

Three things im grateful for:

1. _____
2. _____
3. _____

Three goals for today:

1. _____
2. _____
3. _____

EVENING ENTRY

Goals Met
1 - 3

Energy Level
1 - 5

This Evening I Feel...?

Today I was anxious about...

_____
_____
_____

Three positive things about my day were...

1 _____
2 _____
3 _____

Journal Entry/Free Space...

_____
_____
_____
_____

Today's date is ___/___/___

MORNING ENTRY

Hours Slept

Energy Level
1 - 5

Today I Feel...?

Three things im grateful for :

1. _____
2. _____
3. _____

Three goals for today :

1. _____
2. _____
3. _____

EVENING ENTRY

Goals Met
1 - 3

Energy Level
1 - 5

This Evening I Feel...?

Today I was anxious about...

_____
_____
_____
_____

Three positive things about my day were...

1 _____
2 _____
3 _____

Journal Entry/Free Space...

_____
_____
_____
_____
_____

Today's date is ___/___/___

MORNING ENTRY

Hours Slept	Energy Level 1-5	Today I Feel...?

Three things im grateful for :

1. _____
2. _____
3. _____

Three goals for today :

1. _____
2. _____
3. _____

EVENING ENTRY

Goals Met
1 - 3

Energy Level
1 - 5

This Evening I Feel...?

Today I was anxious about...

_____
_____
_____

Three positive things about my day were...

1. _____
2. _____
3. _____

Journal Entry/Free Space...

_____
_____
_____
_____
_____

Today's date is ___/___/___

MORNING ENTRY

| Hours Slept | Energy Level 1-5 | Today I Feel...? |

Three things im grateful for :

1. _____
2. _____
3. _____

Three goals for today :

1. _____
2. _____
3. _____

EVENING ENTRY

Goals Met
1 - 3

Energy Level
1 - 5

This Evening I Feel...?

Today I was anxious about...

Three positive things about my day were...

1
2
3

Journal Entry/Free Space...

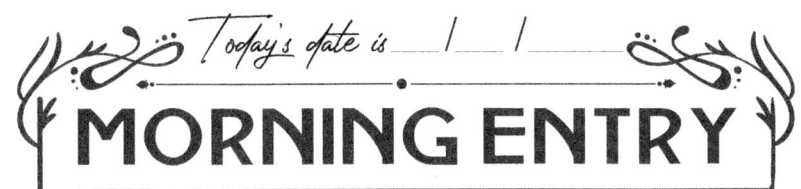

MORNING ENTRY

Today's date is ___/___/___

Hours Slept

Energy Level 1 - 5

Today I Feel...?

Three things im grateful for :

1. _____
2. _____
3. _____

Three goals for today :

1. _____
2. _____
3. _____

EVENING ENTRY

Goals Met
1 - 3

Energy Level
1 - 5

This Evening I Feel...?

Today I was anxious about...

Three positive things about my day were...

1
2
3

Journal Entry/Free Space...

Today's date is ___/___/___

MORNING ENTRY

Hours Slept

Energy Level
1 - 5

Today I Feel...?

Three things im grateful for :

1. _____
2. _____
3. _____

Three goals for today :

1. _____
2. _____
3. _____

EVENING ENTRY

| Goals Met 1-3 | Energy Level 1-5 | This Evening I Feel...? |

Today I was anxious about...

_____
_____
_____

Three positive things about my day were...

1. _____
2. _____
3. _____

Journal Entry/Free Space...

_____
_____
_____
_____
_____

Today's date is ___/___/___

MORNING ENTRY

Hours Slept

Energy Level
1 - 5

Today I Feel...?

Three things im grateful for :

1. _____
2. _____
3. _____

Three goals for today :

1. _____
2. _____
3. _____

EVENING ENTRY

Goals Met
1 - 3

Energy Level
1 - 5

This Evening I Feel...?

Today I was anxious about...

Three positive things about my day were...

1
2
3

Journal Entry/Free Space...

Today's date is ___/___/___

MORNING ENTRY

Hours Slept

Energy Level
1 - 5

Today I Feel...?

Three things im grateful for :

1. _____
2. _____
3. _____

Three goals for today :

1. _____
2. _____
3. _____

EVENING ENTRY

Goals Met
1 - 3

Energy Level
1 - 5

This Evening I Feel...?

Today I was anxious about...

_____
_____
_____

Three positive things about my day were...

1 _____
2 _____
3 _____

Journal Entry/Free Space...

_____
_____
_____
_____

Today's date is ___/___/___

MORNING ENTRY

Hours Slept

Energy Level
1 - 5

Today I Feel...?

Three things im grateful for :

1. _____
2. _____
3. _____

Three goals for today :

1. _____
2. _____
3. _____

EVENING ENTRY

Goals Met
1 - 3

Energy Level
1 - 5

This Evening I Feel...?

Today I was anxious about...

Three positive things about my day were...

1
2
3

Journal Entry/Free Space...

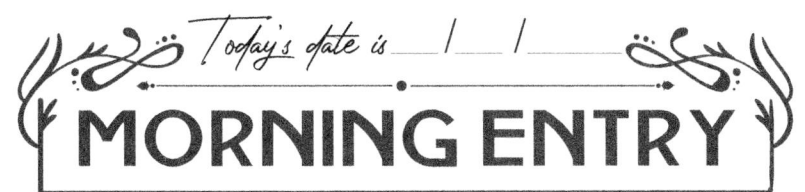

Today's date is ___/___/___

MORNING ENTRY

Hours Slept

Energy Level
1 - 5

Today I Feel...?

Three things im grateful for :

1. _____
2. _____
3. _____

Three goals for today :

1. _____
2. _____
3. _____

EVENING ENTRY

Goals Met
1 - 3

Energy Level
1 - 5

This Evening I Feel...?

Today I was anxious about...

Three positive things about my day were...

1
2
3

Journal Entry/Free Space...

Today's date is ___/___/___

MORNING ENTRY

Hours Slept

Energy Level
1 - 5

Today I Feel...?

Three things im grateful for :

1. _____
2. _____
3. _____

Three goals for today :

1. _____
2. _____
3. _____

EVENING ENTRY

Goals Met
1 - 3

Energy Level
1 - 5

This Evening I Feel...?

Today I was anxious about...

_____
_____
_____

Three positive things about my day were...

1 _____
2 _____
3 _____

Journal Entry/Free Space...

_____
_____
_____
_____
_____

Today's date is ___/___/___

MORNING ENTRY

Hours Slept

Energy Level
1 - 5

Today I Feel...?

✦ *Three things im grateful for* : ✦

1 _____
2 _____
3 _____

☀ ☀ *Three goals for today* : ☀ ☀

1 _____
2 _____
3 _____

EVENING ENTRY

Goals Met
1 - 3

Energy Level
1 - 5

This Evening I Feel...?

Today I was anxious about...

___

Three positive things about my day were...

1. ___
2. ___
3. ___

Journal Entry/Free Space...

___

Today's date is ___/___/___

MORNING ENTRY

Hours Slept

Energy Level
1 - 5

Today I Feel...?

Three things im grateful for :

1 _____
2 _____
3 _____

Three goals for today :

1 _____
2 _____
3 _____

EVENING ENTRY

Goals Met
1 - 3

Energy Level
1 - 5

This Evening I Feel...?

Today I was anxious about...

_____
_____
_____
_____

Three positive things about my day were...

1 _____
2 _____
3 _____

Journal Entry/Free Space...

_____
_____
_____
_____

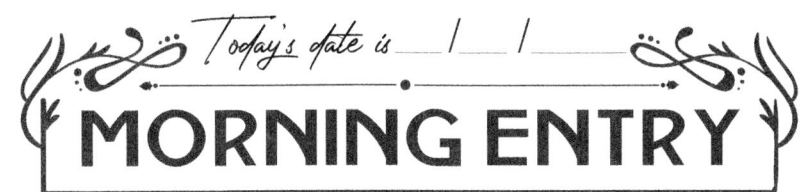
Today's date is ___/___/___

MORNING ENTRY

Hours Slept | **Energy Level** 1 - 5 | **Today I Feel...?**

Three things im grateful for :

1. _____
2. _____
3. _____

Three goals for today :

1. _____
2. _____
3. _____

EVENING ENTRY

Goals Met
1 - 3

Energy Level
1 - 5

This Evening I Feel...?

Today I was anxious about...

Three positive things about my day were...
1
2
3

Journal Entry/Free Space...

Today's date is ___/___/___

MORNING ENTRY

Hours Slept

Energy Level
1 - 5

Today I Feel...?

Three things i'm grateful for :

1. _____
2. _____
3. _____

Three goals for today :

1. _____
2. _____
3. _____

EVENING ENTRY

Goals Met
1 - 3

Energy Level
1 - 5

This Evening I Feel...?

Today I was anxious about...

_____
_____
_____
_____

Three positive things about my day were...

1 _____
2 _____
3 _____

Journal Entry/Free Space...

_____
_____
_____
_____
_____

Today's date is ___/___/___

MORNING ENTRY

Hours Slept

Energy Level
1 - 5

Today I Feel...?

Three things im grateful for :

1. _____
2. _____
3. _____

Three goals for today :

1. _____
2. _____
3. _____

EVENING ENTRY

Goals Met
1 - 3

Energy Level
1 - 5

This Evening I Feel...?

Today I was anxious about...

Three positive things about my day were...

1
2
3

Journal Entry/Free Space...

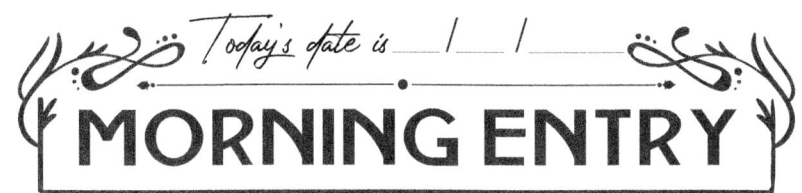

Today's date is ___/___/___

MORNING ENTRY

Hours Slept

Energy Level 1 - 5

Today I Feel...?

Three things im grateful for :

1. _____
2. _____
3. _____

Three goals for today :

1. _____
2. _____
3. _____

EVENING ENTRY

Goals Met
1 - 3

Energy Level
1 - 5

This Evening I Feel...?

Today I was anxious about...

_____
_____
_____
_____

Three positive things about my day were...

1 _____
2 _____
3 _____

Journal Entry/Free Space...

_____
_____
_____
_____
_____

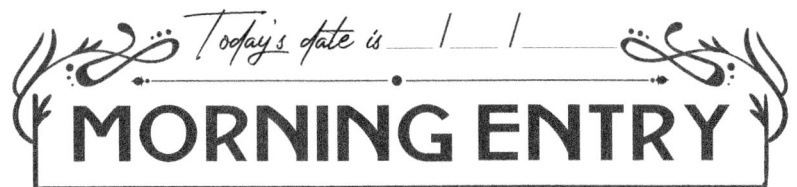

Today's date is ___/___/___

MORNING ENTRY

Hours Slept

Energy Level
1 - 5

Today I Feel...?

✦ Three things im grateful for : ✦

1. _____
2. _____
3. _____

☀ ☀ Three goals for today : ☀ ☀

1. _____
2. _____
3. _____

EVENING ENTRY

Goals Met
1 - 3

Energy Level
1 - 5

This Evening I Feel...?

Today I was anxious about...

_____
_____
_____
_____

Three positive things about my day were...

1 _____
2 _____
3 _____

Journal Entry/Free Space...

_____
_____
_____
_____
_____

Today's date is ___/___/___

MORNING ENTRY

Hours Slept

Energy Level
1 - 5

Today I Feel...?

Three things im grateful for:

1. _____
2. _____
3. _____

Three goals for today:

1. _____
2. _____
3. _____

EVENING ENTRY

Goals Met
1 - 3

Energy Level
1 - 5

This Evening I Feel...?

Today I was anxious about...

_____
_____
_____
_____

Three positive things about my day were...

1 _____
2 _____
3 _____

Journal Entry/Free Space...

_____
_____
_____
_____
_____

Today's date is ___/___/___

MORNING ENTRY

Hours Slept

Energy Level
1 - 5

Today I Feel...?

Three things im grateful for :

1. _____
2. _____
3. _____

Three goals for today :

1. _____
2. _____
3. _____

EVENING ENTRY

Goals Met
1 - 3

Energy Level
1 - 5

This Evening I Feel...?

Today I was anxious about...

Three positive things about my day were...
1
2
3

Journal Entry/Free Space...

Today's date is __/__/____

MORNING ENTRY

Hours Slept

Energy Level
1 - 5

Today I Feel...?

Three things im grateful for :

1. _____
2. _____
3. _____

Three goals for today :

1. _____
2. _____
3. _____

EVENING ENTRY

Goals Met
1 - 3

Energy Level
1 - 5

This Evening I Feel...?

Today I was anxious about...

Three positive things about my day were...

1
2
3

Journal Entry/Free Space...

Today's date is ___/___/___

MORNING ENTRY

Hours Slept

Energy Level
1 - 5

Today I Feel...?

Three things im grateful for :

1. _____
2. _____
3. _____

Three goals for today :

1. _____
2. _____
3. _____

EVENING ENTRY

Goals Met
1 - 3

Energy Level
1 - 5

This Evening I Feel...?

Today I was anxious about...

_____
_____
_____

Three positive things about my day were...

1 _____
2 _____
3 _____

Journal Entry/Free Space...

_____
_____
_____
_____

Today's date is ___ / ___ / ___

MORNING ENTRY

Hours Slept

Energy Level
1 - 5

Today I Feel...?

Three things im grateful for :

1. _____
2. _____
3. _____

Three goals for today :

1. _____
2. _____
3. _____

EVENING ENTRY

Goals Met
1 - 3

Energy Level
1 - 5

This Evening I Feel...?

Today I was anxious about...

_____
_____
_____
_____

Three positive things about my day were...

1 _____
2 _____
3 _____

Journal Entry/Free Space...

_____
_____
_____
_____
_____
_____

Today's date is ___/___/___

MORNING ENTRY

Hours Slept | **Energy Level** 1-5 | **Today I Feel...?**

Three things im grateful for :

1 _____
2 _____
3 _____

Three goals for today :

1 _____
2 _____
3 _____

EVENING ENTRY

Goals Met
1 - 3

Energy Level
1 - 5

This Evening I Feel...?

Today I was anxious about...
___
___
___

Three positive things about my day were...
1 ___
2 ___
3 ___

Journal Entry/Free Space...
___
___
___
___

Today's date is ___/___/___

MORNING ENTRY

Hours Slept

Energy Level
1 - 5

Today I Feel...?

Three things im grateful for :

1. _____
2. _____
3. _____

Three goals for today :

1. _____
2. _____
3. _____

EVENING ENTRY

Goals Met
1 - 3

Energy Level
1 - 5

This Evening I Feel...?

Today I was anxious about...

Three positive things about my day were...
1
2
3

Journal Entry/Free Space...

Today's date is ___/___/___

MORNING ENTRY

Hours Slept

Energy Level 1 - 5

Today I Feel...?

Three things im grateful for :

1. ___
2. ___
3. ___

Three goals for today :

1. ___
2. ___
3. ___

EVENING ENTRY

Goals Met
1 - 3

Energy Level
1 - 5

This Evening I Feel...?

Today I was anxious about...

_____
_____
_____
_____

Three positive things about my day were...

1 _____
2 _____
3 _____

Journal Entry/Free Space...

_____
_____
_____
_____
_____

Today's date is ___/___/___

MORNING ENTRY

Hours Slept

Energy Level
1 - 5

Today I Feel...?

Three things im grateful for :

1. _____
2. _____
3. _____

Three goals for today :

1. _____
2. _____
3. _____

EVENING ENTRY

Goals Met
1 - 3

Energy Level
1 - 5

This Evening I Feel...?

Today I was anxious about...

_____
_____
_____

Three positive things about my day were...

1 _____
2 _____
3 _____

Journal Entry/Free Space...

_____
_____
_____
_____
_____

Today's date is ___/___/___

MORNING ENTRY

Hours Slept

Energy Level
1 - 5

Today I Feel...?

Three things i'm grateful for:

1. _____
2. _____
3. _____

Three goals for today:

1. _____
2. _____
3. _____

EVENING ENTRY

Goals Met
1 - 3

Energy Level
1 - 5

This Evening I Feel...?

Today I was anxious about...

Three positive things about my day were...

1
2
3

Journal Entry/Free Space...

Today's date is ___/___/___

MORNING ENTRY

Hours Slept

Energy Level
1 - 5

Today I Feel...?

Three things im grateful for :

1. _____
2. _____
3. _____

Three goals for today :

1. _____
2. _____
3. _____

EVENING ENTRY

Goals Met
1 - 3

Energy Level
1 - 5

This Evening I Feel...?

Today I was anxious about...

_____
_____
_____
_____

Three positive things about my day were...

1 _____
2 _____
3 _____

Journal Entry/Free Space...

_____
_____
_____
_____
_____

Today's date is ___/___/___

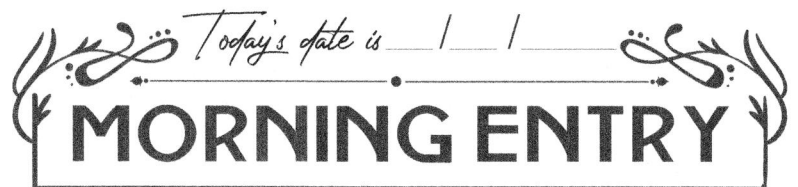

MORNING ENTRY

Hours Slept

Energy Level
1 - 5

Today I Feel...?

Three things im grateful for :

1 _____
  _____

2 _____
  _____

3 _____
  _____

Three goals for today :

1 _____
  _____

2 _____
  _____

3 _____
  _____

EVENING ENTRY

Goals Met	Energy Level	This Evening I Feel...?
1 - 3	1 - 5	

Today I was anxious about...

_____
_____
_____

Three positive things about my day were...

1 _____
2 _____
3 _____

Journal Entry/Free Space...

_____
_____
_____
_____
_____

Today's date is ___/___/___

MORNING ENTRY

Hours Slept

Energy Level
1 - 5

Today I Feel...?

Three things im grateful for:

1 _____
2 _____
3 _____

Three goals for today:

1 _____
2 _____
3 _____

EVENING ENTRY

Goals Met
1 - 3

Energy Level
1 - 5

This Evening I Feel...?

Today I was anxious about...

_____
_____
_____

Three positive things about my day were...

1 _____
2 _____
3 _____

Journal Entry/Free Space...

_____
_____
_____
_____

Today's date is ___/___/___

MORNING ENTRY

Hours Slept

Energy Level
1 - 5

Today I Feel...?

Three things im grateful for :

1 _____
2 _____
3 _____

Three goals for today :

1 _____
2 _____
3 _____

EVENING ENTRY

Goals Met
1 - 3

Energy Level
1 - 5

This Evening I Feel...?

Today I was anxious about...

_____
_____
_____
_____

Three positive things about my day were...

1 _____
2 _____
3 _____

Journal Entry/Free Space...

_____
_____
_____
_____
_____

Today's date is ___/___/___

MORNING ENTRY

Hours Slept

Energy Level
1 - 5

Today I Feel...?

Three things im grateful for :

1. _____
2. _____
3. _____

Three goals for today :

1. _____
2. _____
3. _____

EVENING ENTRY

Goals Met
1 - 3

Energy Level
1 - 5

This Evening I Feel...?

Today I was anxious about...

_____
_____
_____
_____

Three positive things about my day were...

1 _____
2 _____
3 _____

Journal Entry/Free Space...

_____
_____
_____
_____
_____

Today's date is ___/___/___

MORNING ENTRY

Hours Slept

Energy Level
1 - 5

Today I Feel...?

Three things im grateful for:

1. _____
2. _____
3. _____

Three goals for today:

1. _____
2. _____
3. _____

EVENING ENTRY

Goals Met
1 - 3

Energy Level
1 - 5

This Evening I Feel...?

Today I was anxious about...

Three positive things about my day were...

1
2
3

Journal Entry/Free Space...

NOTES

NOTES

NOTES

Printed in Great Britain
by Amazon